PAPERBACK **PLUS**

W9-CDW-755

Table of Contents

Meet Ann Morris

Ann Morris lives in New York City. She loves to ride her bike. When she rides, she always wears a special kind of hat. Do you know why?

Meet Ken Heyman

Ken Heyman likes to travel, and it's a good thing he does. He is a photographer, and he takes pictures all over the world. He has taken pictures in more than sixty different countries!

ANN MORRIS

HATS · HATS · HATS

PHOTOGRAPHS BY
KEN HEYMAN

HOUGHTON MIFFLIN COMPANY
BOSTON
ATLANTA   DALLAS   GENEVA, ILLINOIS   PALO ALTO   PRINCETON

Acknowledgments

For each of the selections listed below, grateful acknowledgment is made for permission to excerpt and/or reprint original or copyrighted materials, as follows:

Selections

Hats, Hats, Hats, by Ann Morris. Copyright © 1989 by Ann Morris. Photography copyright © 1989 by Ken Heyman. Reprinted by permission of William Morrow & Company.

"Make a Paper Hat," adapted from March 1989 *Chickadee* magazine. Copyright © 1989 by The Young Naturalist Foundation. Reprinted by permission.

"My Hat," from *The Eentsy Weentsy Spider: Fingerplays and Action Rhymes,* by Joanna Cole and Stephanie Calmenson. Text copyright © 1991 by Joanna Cole and Stephanie Calmenson. Illustrations copyright © 1991 by Alan Tiegreen. Reprinted by permission of William Morrow & Company.

Illustration

30–31 Christine Czernota.

Photography

i, ii, iii Tony Scarpetta. **ii** © Ken Heyman/Courtesy of Ann Morris. **34** *Chickadee* magazine (t) (b). **35** Mulberry Books (t). **36** Gift of Ruth Carter Stevenson in honor of Adelyn Dohme Breeskin, Trustee, Amon Carter Museum, 1971–1982.

1997 Impression
Houghton Mifflin Edition, 1996

Printed in the U.S.A.

ISBN: 0-395-73213-1

789-B-99 98 97

HATS · HATS · HATS

6

The world is
full of hats.

Soft hats

Hard hats

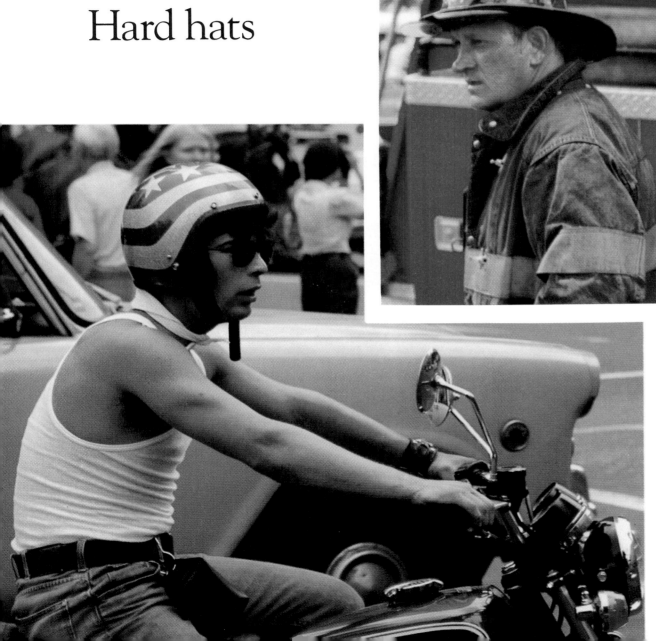

11

Sun hats

14

Fun hats

15

Work hats

Play hats

Ten-gallon cowboy hats

Snuggly
warm hats

22

Scarves and hoods make hats too.

24

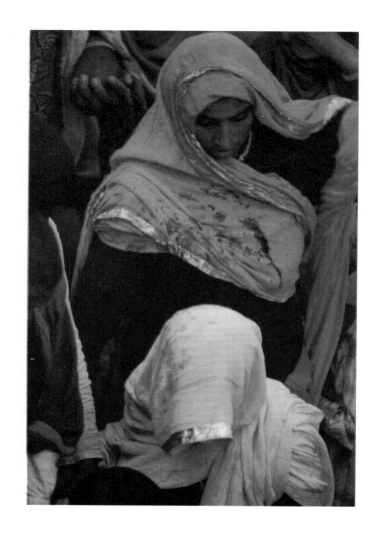

Cover the head

26

Beautiful!

The World We Share

The hats you just read about come from many countries. Use the map to find where these countries are.

Nigeria

United States

ANN MORRIS

HATS
HATS
HATS

PHOTOGRAPHS BY
KEN HEYMAN

Japan

France

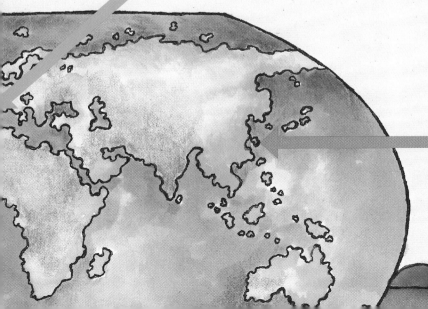

31

Republic of Maldives

Flags
and Stamps

Every country of the world has its own flag. Many have stars, stripes, and other shapes like the ones you see here.

Look at the people on the stamps. Can you see what most of them have on their heads?

10½P
Cycling 1878-1978

United States

Tom Sawyer

United States **8c**

Great Britain

Germany

DEUTSCHE BUNDESPOST BERLIN

10 +5

WOHLFAHRTSMARKE 1970

Kasperl

Make a Paper Hat

Here's how!
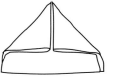

1 Fold one sheet of newspaper in half.

2 Fold the top corners so they meet.

3 Fold one of the bottom flaps in half.

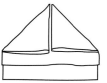
4 Then fold it up again.

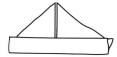
5 Do the same for the other side.

MY HAT

TAP TAP TAP

1 My hat it has three corners,

2 Three corners has my hat.

SHAKE HEAD

3 And had it not three corners,

4 It would not be my hat.

Mother and Daughter, Both Wearing Large Hats

by Mary Cassatt

Mary Cassatt liked to paint pictures of families. She painted *Mother and Daughter, Both Wearing Large Hats* about one hundred years ago. In those days, women and girls often wore fancy hats.